STEVE VINSOl

EGYPTIAN BOATS
AND SHIPS

SHIRE EGYPTOLOGY

Cover illustration
Papyrus fragment C2033,
Museo Egizio, Turin.
(Photograph by courtesy of the Museo Egizio.)

British Library Cataloguing in Publication Data:
Vinson, Steve
Egyptian Boats and Ships.
— Shire Egyptology Series; No. 20
I. Title. II. Series
623. 80932
ISBN 0-7478-0222-X

Published in 1994 by
SHIRE PUBLICATIONS LTD
Cromwell House, Church Street, Princes Risborough,
Buckinghamshire HP27 9AJ, UK.

Series Editor: Barbara Adams

ISBN 0 7478 0222 X

First edition 1994

Printed in Great Britain by
CIT Printing Services, Press Buildings,
Merlins Bridge, Haverfordwest, Dyfed SA61 1XF.

Contents

Acknowledgements

It is a pleasure to acknowledge all those who have helped me in the preparation of this book. First of all I must thank Mrs Barbara Adams, curator at the Petrie Museum of Egyptian Archaeology at University College London and Series Editor. I am indebted to Mr Stéphane Cattaui for permission to publish the relief in figure 29. A glance at the illustration captions will make clear the extent to which other scholars and institutions have helped me in the long process of gathering illustrations; in addition, Harold Dinkel and Helena Jaeschke prepared the original drawings in the book. Professors George F. Bass, D. L. Hamilton, J. Richard Steffy and F. J. van Doorninck of the Nautical Archaeology Program at Texas A&M University deserve special mention, as it was they who introduced me to the study of ancient boats and ships and encouraged me in the direction of Egyptology; Professors Betsy M. Bryan and Hans Goedicke of the Near Eastern Studies Department of The Johns Hopkins University provided welcome assistance and advice as well. Acknowledgement is also made to W. J. Murnane and Penguin Books for the chronology. Finally, I wish to thank my wife, Asma Afsaruddin, not only for her help with the project, but for her unfailing support, encouragement and love.

List of illustrations

Chronology

Based on W. J. Murnane, *The Penguin Guide to Ancient Egypt,* 1983.   An asterisk (*) denotes the archaeological existence of a boat or boat fragments.

Predynastic	5500-3050 BC	
	5500-4000	Badarian
	4000-3500	Naqada I/Amratian
	3500-3300	Naqada II/Gerzean
	3300-3050	Naqada III/Late Predynastic
Early Dynastic	3050-2613 BC	
	3050-2890	Dynasty I*
	2890-2686	Dynasty II
	2686-2613	Dynasty III
Old Kingdom	2613-2181 BC	
	2613-2498	Dynasty IV*
	2498-2345	Dynasty V
	2345-2181	Dynasty VI
First Intermediate Period	2181-2040 BC	
	2181-2040	Dynasties VII-X
	2134-2060	Dynasty XI (Theban)
Middle Kingdom	2040-1782 BC	
	2060-1991	Dynasty XI
	1991-1782	Dynasty XII*
Second Intermediate Period	1782-1570 BC	
	1782-1650	Dynasties XIII and XIV (Egyptian)
	1663-1555	Dynasties XV and XVI (Hyksos)
	1663-1570	Dynasty XVII (Theban)
New Kingdom	1570-1070 BC	
	1570-1293	Dynasty XVIII
	1293-1185	Dynasty XIX
	1185-1070	Dynasty XX
Third Intermediate Period	1070-713 BC	
	1070-945	Dynasty XXI
	945-712	Dynasty XXII
	828-712	Dynasty XXIII
	724-713	Dynasty XXIV

Late Period	713-332 BC	
	713-656	Dynasty XXV (Nubian)
	664-525	Dynasty XXVI
	525-404	Dynasty XXVII (Persian)*
	404-399	Dynasty XXVIII
	399-380	Dynasty XXIX
	380-343	Dynasty XXX (Egyptian/Persian)
Graeco-Roman Period	332 BC to AD 395	
	332-30 BC	Ptolemies
	30 BC - AD 395	Roman Emperors

1
Introduction

Of all the ancient civilisations of the Near East, Egypt was unique in its cultural unity, economic prosperity and political stability. This was made possible by the Nile, a natural highway that linked Egypt together within the protection of the desert.

But a highway is worthless without a vehicle to exploit it. It was the development of boats and ships that turned the Nile into the connecting link that bound the country together. It is probably no coincidence that the first great innovation in nautical technology, the sail, came on the eve of Egypt's unification. Boats carried Egyptian armies south into the Sudan and north to Palestine, and officials and tax collectors on their rounds. They carried stone for pyramids or temples. They hauled grain, wine, beer, cattle, oils and other foods from farms to markets. They brought luxury goods from East Africa or the Mediterranean to the royal palaces and temple estates. They were the means by which itinerant traders peddled their goods, and by which common people travelled from village to village. Boats carried the images of the gods from temple to temple, the dead from this world to the next, and the gods themselves across heaven and into the underworld. It is no wonder that one of the good deeds of which a wealthy Egyptian loved to boast was that he had provided a boat for some poor soul who could not afford one of his own.

In Egypt the Nile is a friendly place for sailors. Before the cycle of the Nile flood was stopped by the Aswan High Dam in the 1960s, the Nile flowed at an average speed of 1 knot (1 nautical mile, or 1.85 km, per hour) at low water in the spring, and increased its current speed to around 4 knots at high flood in the autumn. It is one of the few of the world's great rivers that flows from south to north, making travel easy in that direction. And for most of the year, the wind blows from north to south, making it possible to sail from the Mediterranean more or less continuously almost 900 km to the First Cataract at Aswan. The Nile lacks the storms of the Mediterranean, though even today trick winds occasionally cause overloaded boats to capsize, as they no doubt did in the past.

Within the area historically controlled by Egypt, the most important obstruction to navigation was the rapids of the First Cataract at Aswan. The cataract was navigable at high water but difficult during low river, though even then small boats could ascend the rapids if they were pulled from the shore. Attempts were made to deepen the cataract as early as the Sixth Dynasty, but the usual procedure was apparently to remove large boats from the water and drag them alongside the rapids; grooves alongside the river attest to this, as do rock drawings in the area, some probably as much as five thousand years old, which show gangs of men hauling boats with long cables.

The Second Cataract at Wadi Halfa was more difficult. The experience of Giovanni Belzoni, an early nineteenth-century adventurer and antiquarian who discovered the great temple of Ramesses II at Abu Simbel, shows what it must have been like to navigate:

'We ... advanced with our bark till we found ourselves so tossed about by the different currents and eddies, as to prevent our farther progress; and at the same time were so situated, that we could not return back, for fear of being driven against some of the rocks ... At last we were caught on a sudden in one of the eddies of water, and driven against a rock concealed about two feet below the surface. The shock was terrible; and I must confess, having Mrs Belzoni on board, I felt no small degree of alarm, as I thought the boat was split in two. ... However, as it pleased God, and to my astonishment, there was no harm done.'

Aside from the Nile proper, Egypt has always had an intricate system of waterworks and canals, some designed for irrigation, others for transport. Egypt's system of basin irrigation, practised from antiquity until the High Dam eliminated the flood, was designed to bring water via canals into large basins and hold it there for forty to sixty days to let the river's silt settle. Once this was done, the water was let out and the silt-rich fields were sown; but while the basins were full, villages were surrounded by water 1 to 2 metres deep, perched on mounds that reminded the Greek historian Herodotus of Aegean islands. At such times boats were indispensable.

Other major canals or waterworks were designed expressly for transport. The earliest record of dredging the First Cataract — the shallow rapids at Aswan — goes back to the Sixth Dynasty, c.2400 BC. The great city of Memphis, capital in the Old Kingdom and site of one of the chief ports and shipyards of the New Kingdom, was probably connected by canals to the necropolis at Giza; these canals were indispensable for getting construction material to the site where the pyramids were being built.

In the New Kingdom, the presence of a major canal east of the Delta is recorded in reliefs of the Nineteenth Dynasty Pharaoh Seti I, which show him and his army crossing it after a foray into Palestine (figure 1). Late in Egyptian history, the Pharaoh Necho began a canal from the Nile to the Red Sea, a project that was not completed until the conquest of Egypt by the Persians. In its heyday, Herodotus reported that some of the largest ships of the time could navigate the canal two abreast.

Other major constructions for the use of boats and ships included artificial harbours, small ones at temples for the use of ceremonial boats, but other quite large ones for the use of river-borne commerce. The pyramids seem to have been served by harbours connected to the great canal of Memphis. Those small ports served both the needs of the builders and the later ceremonial needs of the priests who worshipped the Pharaohs buried there. Towns and villages probably had 'port' areas that consisted of a rocky jetty built a short way out into the Nile, or simply a stretch of sandy beach.

Though there are many representations of boats unloading or taking on cargo, the best-preserved pictorial representation of an entire harbour is a tomb painting of the port of Akhetaten, the capital of the Eighteenth Dynasty heretic Pharaoh Akhenaten. Here are visible all the activities that must have been associated with riverboats: the loading and discharging of cargo, the repair of equipment, and storage of spare parts like masts and oars.

One of the few well-explored archaeological remnants of a pre-classical commercial harbour is the Birket Habu, a huge basin on the west bank of the Nile opposite the modern city of Luxor, ancient Thebes. The Birket Habu was built during the reign of the Eighteenth Dynasty pharaoh Amenophis III, father of Akhenaten. The harbour, which today is completely dry and marked by the huge mounds of earth dug from it by its builders, was excavated in the early 1970s by Barry Kemp and David O'Connor. According to its excavators, it had an area of at least

1. Seti I crossing the border between Egypt and Asia. (From *The Battle Reliefs of King Sety I*, The University of Chicago Oriental Institute Publications volume 107, Reliefs and Inscriptions at Karnak volume 4, plate 6. Reproduced courtesy of the Oriental Institute of the University of Chicago.)

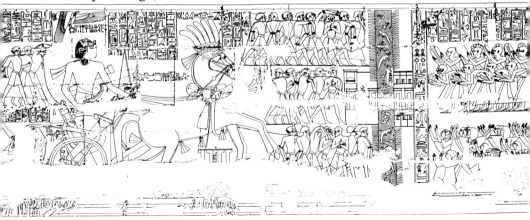

2.4 million square metres. The depth is uncertain but in order to handle ships at all times of the year it would have had to be at least 8 metres. Kemp and O'Connor doubt that the harbour was dug so deeply and believe it probably could not have handled large ships during the period from February to July, when the river was low.

Other major harbours known from Egyptian literature included the Per-Nefer, the harbour of Memphis, where the royal dockyards of Tuthmosis III were, and the Delta port of Tanis, from which voyages such as the famous trip of Wenamun were begun. On the Red Sea coast, voyages to Punt were launched from a harbour at present-day Quseir as early as the Middle Kingdom. In the Graeco-Roman period Berenike, further south, was the home port for Greek sailors bound for East Africa, Arabia and India, though Quseir continued in use. The Egyptians seem not to have had any ports on the Mediterranean coast before the end of the New Kingdom, and the harbour of Alexandria was not developed until Egypt's conquest by Alexander the Great. However, there do appear to have been settlements along the Mediterranean coast used by foreign traders, who probably also came up river at times to trade in Egypt proper. One such site is at Marsah Matruh, about halfway between Alexandria and the modern border between Egypt and Libya. Here, the presence of foreigners is marked by large quantities of pottery from Cyprus and Syria-Palestine, dating to the late Eighteenth or early Nineteenth Dynasty. How important such settlements were has not yet become clear.

2
Before the Old Kingdom

Egypt was inhabited as early as the Palaeolithic Period, and it is difficult to believe that there was ever a time when humans failed to take advantage of the ubiquitous papyrus to build rafts or floats. Nevertheless, our evidence for the use of boats in Egypt does not begin until almost the end of prehistory, between 6000 and 5000 BC.

The oldest datable boat representations are models. The very oldest seems to be from the Neolithic site of Merimda Beni Salaam. Others almost as old come from the Badarian culture of Upper Egypt, *c.*5500 to 4000 BC (figure 2). These are models of true boats, with built-up sides — but it seems most likely that the boats they represented were made of papyrus bundles, not wood. This is because there is no evidence that at this period carpentry skills were advanced enough to build planked boats, and Egypt never had enough large straight trees to build dug-out canoes.

The next phase of Egyptian prehistory, called the Amratian Period by some authors and the Naqada I Period by others, has left various representations of boats — models, vase paintings and others. Like their forerunners of the Neolithic and Badarian Period, Amratian models also appear to be of papyrus boats, since they seem to have bundles of papyrus painted on their sides. These are canoe-shaped, with flat bottoms. Some boats from the Gerzean (Naqada II) Period (*c.*3500-3300 BC), have the papyrus bundles modelled on them.

Beginning in the Amratian Period, there are many drawings of large rafts that, because they have up-curving bow and stem posts that narrow to a point, seem to be made of papyrus. This recalls the traditional

2. Badarian boat model. (Photograph courtesy of the Petrie Museum of Egyptian Archaeology, University College London. UC 9024.)

African method of making papyrus rafts, described by Björn Landström in his *Ships of the Pharaohs*, in which the raft-builder starts with a broom-shaped bundle of reeds and then gradually widens it until his raft reaches its desired mid-ship breadth. The earliest datable representation of this type of vessel is a crude charcoal drawing scratched on a dried-mud box, which comes from a late Amratian grave (figure 3); most similar rafts are seen in rock drawings.

3. Amratian drawing of a papyrus raft. (Drawing by Harold Dinkel after D. Randall-MacIver and A. C. Mace, *El Amrah and Abydos* [London, 1902], plate XII.)

It is only at the beginning of the Gerzean/Naqada II Period that there is reason to believe that wooden boats were being built in Egypt. Indirect evidence comes from the fact that the graves of the Gerzean Period contain the first indication that carpentry was sufficiently advanced for the building of planked boats. Buried in some of the richer graves are copper woodworking tools, such as axes, adzes and chisels. The beginning of the Gerzean Period also furnishes the first examples of wooden planks, which were cut in a wide variety of lengths, widths and thicknesses.

The planks from this period that have been found by archaeologists were used either in primitive coffins, or as simple walls or roofs to keep dirt from falling in on the body. When the planks were joined together it was always by lashing, which was the normal method in ancient Egypt of fastening boat planks together. This shows that even at this period carpenters were developing the basic techniques they needed to construct wooden boats.

The early Gerzean Period also marked the first appearance of a new type of boat in Egyptian art. This is the so-called 'sickle-shaped' boat (figure 4), best-known from paintings on vases but also known from petroglyphs, models, and even the only known painted tomb from the Predynastic Period. Sickle-shaped boats look distinctly different from the papyrus rafts already described, because their bows and stems do not narrow to a point. This fact alone suggests that sickle-shaped boats were not made of papyrus bundles. It is probably also significant that this new boat type appears at the same time as the earliest evidence for carpentry skills.

4. Sickle-shaped boat from grave 101 at Gerzeh. (Photograph courtesy of the Petrie Museum of Egyptian Archaeology, University College London. UC. 10769.)

Sickle-shaped boats are most often drawn on a particular kind of pot found in richer graves of the Gerzean Period. In these funerary contexts they are shown in a very conventionalised way, with many paddles, two cabins, palm-fronds at the bow and enigmatic standards. Some of these standards have been plausibly linked to religious or provincial emblems known from historic Egypt, but many remain inexplicable.

It is impossible to know to what extent the vessels on the decorated pots were meant to represent boats for the dead and to what extent they mirrored the boats used in everyday life. The fact that similar boats are drawn on rock surfaces throughout Upper Egypt and Nubia seems to show that some such boats were the usual means of transport of the day. Working boats probably lacked the conventional complement of two cabins, a standard and a palm-frond, though the palm-frond might well have been functional, acting as a small sail. Such an arrangement is known from sub-Saharan Africa, and experiments with such proto-sails have shown that they can add as much as 1 knot to the speed of a small boat.

But it seems clear that these boats had some sort of funerary significance. One of the best depictions of the sickle-shaped boats comes from a fresco in the so-called Decorated Tomb at Hierakonpolis in Upper Egypt (figure 5). This extremely faded painting, the oldest tomb painting from Egypt, is in the Cairo Museum. It includes five such boats (and a sixth boat, different in its black colour and the single high post at its bow). They are very like the boats of the decorated pots except that four of them have no paddles, and the fifth has only a single steering paddle.

Because this painting was made before any kind of decipherable writing was developed in Egypt, no one has ever advanced a convincing explanation as to what the artist meant to portray. The uppermost boat has a figure seated in an open cabin or kiosk, which parallels the kiosks seen on historic Egyptian paintings of the voyage of the dead to Abydos. Such funerary voyages were often shown being made in the company

5. Boat procession from Hierakonpolis tomb 100 (the Decorated Tomb). (From J. E. Quibell and F. W. Green, *Hierakonpolis Part II*, Egyptian Research Account, Fifth Memoir [London, 1902], plate LXXV.)

of a small fleet — but on present evidence it would be risky to try to project this historic theme back into prehistory.

Some have seen in the painting the depiction of a naval battle. These would argue that the large black ship with one high end is sailing from left to right, in opposition to the sickle-shaped boats, which are sailing from right to left. This appears not to be the case, however, as will be explained presently when we turn to such high-ended boats. Still other authors have argued that the scene merely shows daily life on the Nile or is a replay of specific events in the life of the chieftain once buried in the tomb. A recent attempt to explain the painting holds that the hunting and fighting was part of a primitive Heb-sed festival, the historic ritual by which an aging Pharaoh renewed his strength and vigour.

From petroglyphs that show men in sickle-shaped boats, it appears that they could be as long as 17 metres or so. One petroglyph shows a gang of about 32 men pulling a boat by ropes and also shows thirty paddles projecting from the hull (figure 6); assuming each paddler needed

6. Petroglyph showing a gang of men hauling a boat (most human figures omitted). (Drawing by Harold Dinkel after G. W. Murray and O. H. Myers, 'Some Predynastic Rock-Drawings', *Journal of Egyptian Archaeology*, 19 [1933], 129-32, figure 1.)

7. Petroglyph of a high-bowed boat. (Drawing by Harold Dinkel after R. Engelmayer, *Die Felsgravierungen im Distrikt Sayala-Nubien 1 Die Schiffdarstellungen* [Vienna, 1965], plate XII.4.)

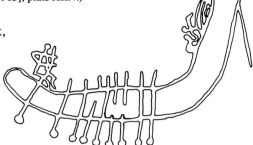

one metre of space to work, and assuming the thirty paddles are meant to indicate the paddles for both sides of the boat, a crew of about 32 working a boat of something over 15 metres seems about right.

A number of petroglyphs of boats with a single high end show a crewman with a steering paddle in the low end, and this would seem to confirm that the high end of the black vessel in the decorated tomb at Hierakonpolis is its bow (figure 7). The black ship also has a palm-frond just behind the bow post, in exactly the same place as the palm-fronds of the sickle-shaped boats. This still leaves us unable to explain the function of the high posts, though it is interesting that they resemble the posts of similarly high-bowed boats from the Early Bronze Age Aegean.

The construction methods of the Predynastic boatwrights are impossible to reconstruct in detail. It seems probable that the planks were somehow lashed together. The boats probably lacked keels, as there is hardly any evidence from archaeology or literature that Egyptian boats ever had keels; whether they had frames or ribs is open to conjecture. It seems likely that the boats were usually made of acacia or sycamore, since these are two of the commonest Egyptian woods and they were common boatbuilding material in later times. Pine and cypress were imported from Syria-Palestine for royal or sacred boats early in Egyptian history, and there is some slight evidence of wood importation as early as the Amratian Period. So far, however, there is no indication that this trade was sufficient for the building of boats.

As early as the Old Kingdom the planks of the funerary boat of the Fourth Dynasty Pharaoh Khufu were joined together with tenons. Tenons, flat tongues of wood designed to fit into edge cuttings called mortises, served mainly to maintain the boat's shape — lashings actually held the planks together. Mortise-and-tenon joinery was in use by the First Dynasty, very probably in boat construction; it is not known whether the planks of Gerzean boats were joined in this way.

Just after the end of the Gerzean Period, in the brief Naqada III Period that immediately preceded the founding of the First Dynasty and the beginning of written history, a radical innovation was seen in Egypt: the sail.

Perhaps the earliest representation of a sailing boat is carved on a stone censer found at the site of Qustul in Egyptian Nubia (figure 8). It shows a new boat type with high bow and stem posts, very different from the sickle-shaped boats that dominated the Gerzean Period. This new angular boat could carry a single square sail set rather far forward. The rigging is not indicated at all, and it is unclear whether the sail had a boom, which was to become a typical feature of sailing tackle in the Nile Valley and the rest of the eastern Mediterranean for the next 1800 years.

The stern posts on boats such as the one on the Qustul censer have a distinctive triangular shape. In the Qustul censer, the sailing ship and the two other similar boats without sails seem to be explicitly identified with a king who is shown riding in them. A very similar boat, though without a sail, is shown on an inscribed wooden tablet of Aha from Abydos, now in the British Museum, either the first or second king of the First Dynasty.

Should these new angular sailing boats be interpreted as the descendants of sickle-shaped boats or as an innovative new technology, perhaps brought by new people? If the latter, people from where? The simplest answer seems to be Upper Egypt or Nubia, since that is where most of the many petroglyphs of this type of boat are to be found. But many authors have drawn parallels between these angular boats and high-ended boats from Mesopotamia. These writers have argued that these are the boats of Sumerian traders or conquerors who sailed around

8. The earliest representation of a sailing boat, carved on the stone censer from Qustul, Nubia. (Drawing by Harold Dinkel after B. Williams, 'The Lost Pharaohs of Nubia', *Archaeology* 33.5 [1980], 16.)

the Arabian peninsula and entered Egypt through the Wadi Hammamat, a natural depression between the Nile and the Red Sea.

It seems very likely that there was some sort of contact between the nascent civilisations of Egypt and Mesopotamia — artistic motifs and new forms of architecture in Egypt do seem to reflect some contact with ancient Sumer. However, there is so far little evidence for direct, seaborne contact. There are few early items of Mesopotamian provenance in Egypt and no Predynastic Egyptian artefacts in Mesopotamia. The oldest Mesopotamian cylinder seals and jars reported from Egypt are older than their oldest counterparts in the southern Persian Gulf, and the latest archaeological investigations have turned up no Sumerian material at all on the Arabian coast beyond the Straits of Hormuz. Mesopotamian records from this early period do mention sea voyages to places identified as Oman and the Indus Valley, but not to Egypt. And in historic times there is no clear-cut evidence for such a sea trade between Egypt and the Persian Gulf until the Graeco-Roman period.

The resemblance between the high-ended Egyptian boats and their supposed Mesopotamian prototypes is superficial at best. For example, the Egyptian bow post is almost always higher and of a different shape than the stern post, while early Sumerian boats are normally perfectly symmetrical fore and aft. Moreover, there are no representations of sailing boats in Sumerian art. In any event, since there are far more representations of high-ended boats in Egypt than there are from Mesopotamia, one might better argue that the boats were invented on the Nile and sailed from there to the east!

There is, however, one piece of compelling evidence in favour of Mesopotamian or Mesopotamian-inspired vessels in Egypt: a carved ivory knife handle from Gebel el-Arak in Upper Egypt (figure 9). The knife handle, now in the Louvre, was not found in an archaeological context but was bought from dealers in the area of Gebel el-Arak. It shows men fighting below registers of boats, some of which have the typical sickle-shaped profile, others of which have high symmetrical posts at bow and stern. These high-ended boats are the only vessels known from Predynastic Egypt that strongly recall Sumerian craft. For the present, the picture remains unclear.

The first good evidence for both the true size of Egyptian boats and their constructional features dates from the First Dynasty. Many of the wealthiest citizens of Egypt had boats buried with them, which presumably they planned to sail in the afterlife. The largest of these boats were buried in the First Dynasty cemeteries at Abydos and Saqqara, though others are known from less well-appointed cemeteries at Helwan. Twelve intact First Dynasty boat burials were discovered in 1991 at Abydos by David O'Connor of the University of Pennsylvania. The

9. The ivory knife handle from Gebel el-Arak. (Drawing by Harold Dinkel. Musée du Louvre E. 11517.)

twelve boat pits, which vary in length from 15 to 18 metres, were found next to one another immediately adjacent to a large mud-brick enclosure wall. So far, only one of the hulls has been partially excavated. A preliminary sounding revealed a hull 1.47 metres wide at the top, 41 cm wide at the bottom, and 41 cm deep, with planks of approximately 10 cm in thickness. Unfortunately no evidence of the techniques used to construct the vessel was uncovered. However, study of this 'fleet', the earliest known planked boats in the world, promises to revolutionise our knowledge of Early Dynastic Egyptian nautical technology. Before this discovery, however, only a single First Dynasty boat burial had been discovered with its boat still in it, from Saqqara, and it was in such poor condition that it was apparently not thought worth preserving and documenting. The holes that the boats were placed in, however, give a rough indication that these craft averaged about 17 metres in length, something less than 3 metres in width at their beam, and about 1.5 metres from bottom plank to sheer line.

No identifiable fragments have come from any of the other First Dynasty boat graves from Saqqara or Helwan, but there seem to have been a few planks from First Dynasty boats buried in graves at the First Dynasty cemetery at Tarkhan, a few miles south of Cairo (figure 10). These planks were used, like planks in Gerzean graves, as parts of coffins or as makeshift roofing material. However, some of them have peculiar V-shaped lashing holes that permitted planks to be literally sewn together — a scheme identical to the lashing system used in the Fourth Dynasty funerary boat of Khufu. Several have mortises in the edge to receive tenons, as also have the edges of the Khufu boat's planks; others are curved and seem likely to have been the ribs or frames of small boats.

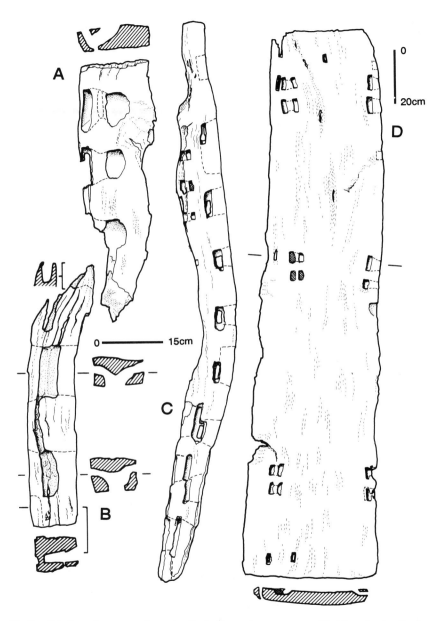

10. Possible boat fragments from the Early Dynastic cemetery at Tarkhan, in the Petrie Museum of Egyptian Archaeology, University College London. (A: UC 17157; B: UC 17156; C: UC 17162; D: UC 17166. Drawing by Helena Jaeschke.)

From this, it seems that the sailing boats of the First Dynasty were more or less the same size as their Gerzean predecessors. They most likely had frames and seem to have used mortise-and-tenon joints, a technology that was to become so important in Mediterranean boat construction that it was to last into the early Middle Ages. They had no keels. However, one or two models do show internal beams in the boats' bilges that might have been intended to prevent 'hogging' or sagging of the boats' ends. This will be examined further in the next chapter.

By the First Dynasty, boats were being used in all the ways that would characterise ships throughout Egyptian history. The Qustul censer shows kings engaged in royal water-borne processions. The painted tomb of Hierakonpolis and the boat graves of Saqqara and Helwan show that boats already played a major part in funerary beliefs. By the late Predynastic Period trade goods from Syria-Palestine are found throughout Egypt, and by the First Dynasty large beams of imported wood are being used in buildings, beams which would have been most easily transportable by sea. Some petroglyphs show cattle aboard ships, showing that, just as in historic Egypt, ships were being used for domestic commerce. A rock inscription of the First Dynasty king Djer, which shows captives tied to the prows of boats, shows that boats were already being used for warfare (figure 11). As Egypt emerges into the full light of history around 3000 BC, there is nothing more important to its power and well-being than its boats and ships.

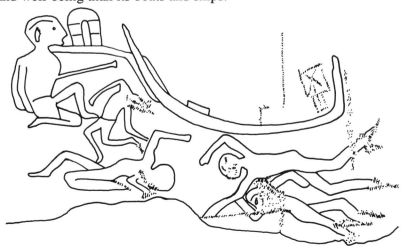

11. Petroglyph of the First Dynasty king Djer. (Drawing by Harold Dinkel after A. J. Arkell, 'Varia Sudanica', *Journal of Egyptian Archaeology* 36 [1950], 24-40, figure 1.)

3
The Old Kingdom

In the Old Kingdom, Egypt became a fully-fledged nautical power. There is little to say about boats and ships of the Third Dynasty, when pyramid building began in Egypt, but by the Fourth Dynasty nearly every feature that was to characterise Egyptian shipbuilding until the end of the New Kingdom seems to have been on its way to full development.

The great surviving masterpiece of Old Kingdom shipbuilding is the funerary boat of Khufu, the builder of the Great Pyramid at Giza (figure 12). Khufu is better known as Cheops, the name used by ancient Greek historians of Egypt. There are actually two such boats, since one lies unexcavated in the pit where it was placed upon the king's death around 2650 BC. But the first Khufu boat, excavated in 1954 and brilliantly reassembled by the Egyptian conservator Hag Ahmed Moustafa, epitomises the technique of the Old Kingdom shipwrights.

The Khufu boat was found in a sealed pit next to the Great Pyramid at Giza. Originally there were five boats buried next to the pyramid, of which all but two had been removed in antiquity. The ship is built primarily of cedar, which must have been imported from Syria-Palestine. (The earliest Egyptian textual reference to sea trade, the Fifth Dynasty Palermo Stone, records the importation of wood by ship from the Levant.) It is 43.3 metres long overall, with a maximum beam of about 5.7 metres and a maximum height from bottom planking to the sheer line of less than 2 metres.

The function of the vessel is still controversial. Some believe that it was a 'solar' boat, intended to take the dead king on journeys through heaven with the sun. Others see it simply as the vessel which ferried the king from his residence to the tomb on his funeral day. Others would argue that it was an official vessel that had been used by the Pharaoh on ceremonial occasions. It is impossible to say whether any of the proposed uses would preclude any of the others — in other words, all these

12. Funerary boat of Khufu. (Copyright National Geographic Society, April 1988, pages 529-33. Photograph by Victor Boswell.)

theories could be correct. Clearly, these fine dimensions would rule out any possibility that it was anything other than a ceremonial vessel of some sort.

In its form and in its constructional details this ship is the linear descendant of the angular ships that made their appearance in the Naqada III Period and First Dynasty. Its straight bow post strongly recalls such boats. The stem decoration has changed to a sickle shape, a shape which was to be typical of Egyptian ceremonial or sacred barques for the remainder of pharaonic civilisation. While its dimensions are much larger than those of the First Dynasty boats buried next to the First Dynasty tombs at Saqqara, the proportions seem about the same: the Khufu boat's length-to-beam ratio is 7.1:1, while the average length-to-beam ratio of the boat graves at Saqqara and Helwan is 7.9:1.

The builders of the Khufu ship used techniques which were established in the First Dynasty. Each plank is held to its neighbours by means of mortise-and-tenon joints, which worked to maintain the shape of the hull. Unlike the ships of classical antiquity, however, the Khufu boat's joinery did not provide the main structural strength; instead, the ship was held together by lashing, which ran laterally through V-shaped holes much like those of some of the Tarkhan planks.

Workmen can be seen assembling ships with mortise-and-tenon joints in a number of Old Kingdom tomb reliefs, among which the most important is that of the Fifth Dynasty courtier Ti at Saqqara. Other reliefs from a slightly later period show that during the construction phase hulls were fitted with cables that ran from bow to stem and were twisted to provide tension. It would appear that boatwrights put their hulls under this tension while lashing them together, effectively 'spring-loading' the hull as a means of keeping the joints and lashings tight.

The Khufu boat also differs from the ships of the Greeks and Romans in its lack of a keel. This lack presented the boatwrights with a major structural problem. It has been estimated that the Khufu boat's waterline length is about 32.5 metres, meaning that about 5 metres of the vessel's total length at each end of the ship would have been left unsupported by water. To keep these ends from sagging under their own weight — a phenomenon called 'hogging' — the boat's builder installed heavy longitudinal girders at deck level, which kept the boat bent into its graceful curve much like a string keeps a bow bent.

In classical antiquity shipwrights employed the keel, which serves both as the foundation from which the ship's planks are built up and, more importantly, as a source of longitudinal stiffening. In later times a second, interior member called a keelson was sometimes added to provide even more rigidity. There is at present no evidence that Egyptian shipwrights ever adopted the keel, though they could use heavy beams to strengthen the hull, certainly at deck level and perhaps in the bilge.

Old Kingdom reliefs, however, show that another important tool to prevent hogging was the 'hogging truss', a heavy cable that ran from bow to stern and helped maintain the boat's curvature. A hogging truss *par excellence* is seen on the ships carved on the walls of the Sun Temple of the Fifth Dynasty Pharaoh Sahure (figure 13). These ships, which are quite different in their profile from the Khufu vessel, are apparently designed for use on the high seas. The inscription accompanying them does not tell us the name the Egyptians gave them, but some sea-going vessels were called 'Byblos ships', after the Syro-Palestinian port of Byblos. It seems likely that Old Kingdom Byblos ships were very like Sahure's ships. These seem to have just returned to Egypt from somewhere in Syria, since on board are clearly shown bearded Syrians bowing to the Pharaoh. Even if Byblos boats were closely identified with Syria-Palestine during the Old Kingdom, the word eventually became completely generic, appearing once in the New Kingdom over a simple funerary barge, and in the Ptolemaic period it was used to describe the warships of the Greeks. And even in the late Old Kingdom Byblos ships were used to trade with Punt, a land on the Red Sea coast of East Africa, perhaps Somalia.

The rigging of Sahure's ships shows a short-lived experiment in Egyptian nautical technology, the bipod mast. While the single-pole mast is the first type seen in Egypt, many Old Kingdom ships were fitted with a bipod mast designed to spread the weight of the sailing tackle over a larger area of the hull than a single-pole mast would have. Similar arrangements are known from nautical traditions as diverse as the reed boats of South America and large wooden ships of late medieval Holland — both of which shared with these early Egyptian ships the

13. Sea-going ships from the Sun Temple of Sahure. (Drawing by Harold Dinkel after L. Borchardt, *Das Grabdenkmal des Königs Sa3hure II* [Osnabruck, 1981; reprint of the original edition, Berlin, 1913], plate 12.)

characteristic flat bottom without a keel. Strangely, however, no bipod mast is seen after the end of the Sixth Dynasty, even though Egyptian ships and boats continued to be flat-bottomed.

Whether boatbuilders used monopod or bipod masts, their sails were hung from yards that could be hoisted and lowered by means of ropes called halyards (figure 14). The sail was kept square with a boom, or lower yard, whose weight was usually supported by ropes called 'lifts'. In the Old Kingdom these lifts were attached to the middle of the mast.

14. Sailing boat from the Fifth Dynasty tomb of Inti at Deshasheh. (From W. M. F. Petrie, *Deshasheh* [London, 1898], plate VI.)

The halyards were tied off in the stern of the boat, along with numerous other ropes called backstays. Old Kingdom boats appear to have had an inordinate number of backstays; their function is obscure but they may have also served to help hold up the stern end of the boat, as well as to provide stability to the mast. In some cases the boom was not held up by lifts but seems to have been simply laid on the deck athwartships. A few Old Kingdom boats show a peculiar triangular sail, but this arrangement apparently had vanished by the Middle Kingdom.

Unlike the graceful curve of the Khufu funerary boat, Nile freight boats were more scow-shaped, with blunt bows and sterns. Reliefs and paintings show such boats of various sizes, with cargo piled precariously high, and steersmen sitting on top of that (figure 15). Papyrus boats and rafts are commonly seen in Old Kingdom tombs, as are scenes of groups of men jousting aboard papyrus skiffs.

The First Dynasty Pharaoh Djer used boats in an attack on Nubian villages as early as 2900 BC, and the use of ships in warfare continued in the Old Kingdom. The tomb autobiography of Weni, a court official under the Sixth Dynasty Pharaoh Pepi I, records an amphibious assault at an obscure place he calls Antelope Nose. In the battle, Weni reportedly trapped rebel tribesmen between a land-based army and a contingent of marines who were ferried to battle on *nemi* ships. *Nemi* ships are mentioned nowhere else in known Egyptian texts but Weni's autobiography.

15. Old Kingdom transport boats. (From C. R. Lepsius, *Denkmaeler aus Aegypten und Aethiopien*, Zweite Abteilung, Bl. 104b.)

Weni made great use of ships in his career, and elsewhere in his autobiography he provides us with more details. On several occasions Weni was dispatched to Upper Egypt or Nubia for granite or alabaster. On one such expedition for granite Weni used two types of boat: *satch* boats and *sekhet* boats, both of which were apparently particular types of cargo ship. Weni made the interesting observation that his *satch* boats were of the 'eight rib' variety. It is tempting to identify these 'ribs' with the boat's internal frames, which are often informally called 'ribs' in English as well. If so, the Khufu boat would be a 'sixteen-rib' vessel, and one could estimate that the 'eight-rib' boats Weni used were about 21 metres long.

Weni does tell us the size of the *sekhet* boats he built during a trip to Upper Egypt to collect alabaster: 60 cubits, or about 32 metres. He claims he was able to have a boat built in seventeen days, using the local acacia wood. *Satch* boats are shown in the pyramid causeway reliefs of the Fifth Dynasty king Unas, where they are carrying pairs of

10.5 metre stone columns laid end to end, again implying a ship of about 30 metres in length.

Another very common boat name in the Old and Middle kingdoms was *depet*. This may well have been no more than a generic word for boat. It appears in an amusing context in the Sixth Dynasty autobiography of Harkhuf. Harkhuf had been sent to Nubia to collect various African commodities early in the reign of Pepi II, then only a boy. Harkhuf's autobiography includes the text of a letter from the young king, who can barely retain his royal dignity in his excitement at Harkhuf's imminent return with a dancing pygmy. Pepi wrote:

'Hurry and bring this pygmy with you, whom you have brought from the land of the horizon-people, alive, sound and healthy, for the dances of the god, to make glad the heart, to make happy the heart of the King of Upper and Lower Egypt Neferkare (may he live forever!). When he goes down with you to the *depet* ship, arrange for excellent men to be around him on deck, so that he does not fall into the water! When he sleeps at night, arrange for excellent men to sleep around him in his tent. Inspect ten times at night! My majesty would love to see this pygmy more than the tribute of the mine lands and of Punt!'

4
The Middle Kingdom

In terms of nautical practice the Middle Kingdom might well be regarded as a transitional period. In general, ships and boats were well on the way to assuming the form they were to have in the New Kingdom, though there were some features unique to the period. The bipod mast disappeared, as did the triangular sail. New hull shapes appeared, which seem to have either influenced or been influenced by developments in the Aegean.

Whilst there are fewer pictorial representations of boats in Middle Kingdom Egyptian art than in Old Kingdom art, the evidence for nautical practices is nevertheless more varied. Aside from paintings and reliefs, large numbers of boat models have come down to us from the Middle Kingdom. Four Middle Kingdom funerary boats are extant, and fragments of boats have been found in the Middle Egyptian sites of Lisht and Lahun and at the Red Sea coastal site of Marsa Gawasis. Marsa Gawasis has also yielded the oldest certain anchors known from Egypt.

Ships and shipping play a major part in one of the great prose compositions of the Middle Kingdom, the Story of the Shipwrecked Sailor. The story is far more fairy tale than ship's log but it does allow us to view Egyptian ships in a context that was familiar to the Egyptians themselves. One other written source of great importance is the dockyard records of the Pharaoh Sesostris I.

The four funerary boats from the Middle Kingdom are part of a group of six excavated at Dahshur by the French Egyptologist Jacques De Morgan. Two of the boats are at the Cairo Museum; one is at the Field Museum at the University of Chicago, and the fourth is at the Carnegie Museum in Pittsburgh. The whereabouts of the last two are unknown.

The Dahshur boats are of a spoon shape that is quite characteristically Egyptian (figure 16). Travellers on the Upper Nile in the nineteenth and twentieth centuries described local boats, called *naggrs*, which were still very close to the Dahshur boats in their size and shapes. The internal construction of the Dahshur boats, however, is very unusual, compared both to other Egyptian boats and to ancient east Mediterranean shipbuilding in general.

The six boats, found buried next to the pyramid of Sesostris III, average about 10 metres long, 2.5 metres wide at maximum beam and 1 metre from bottom plank to sheer line. As in the Khufu boat, mortise-and-tenon joints are used to maintain the shape of the hull, and the hull is tied together with through-beams, the earliest attestation of this

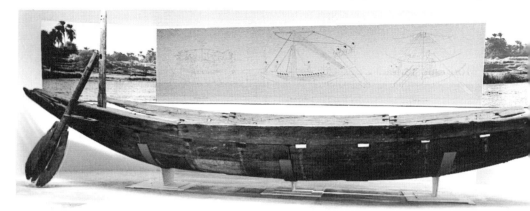

16. The Dahshur boat in Pittsburgh. (Photograph courtesy of the Carnegie Museum of Natural History. CMNH 1842-1.)

important structural device; but unlike the Fourth Dynasty boat, the hull has neither frames nor structural lashings. Instead, planks are attached to one another with clamps shaped like a bow tie, often called 'dovetail' clamps. It has been speculated almost since the Dahshur boats appeared on public view that many, though probably not all, of these dovetail clamps are a modern conservation device. No early drawings or photographs from the 1894 excavation exist to answer the question.

The Dahshur boats' lack of internal framing seems to conform with Herodotus' fifth century BC description of Egyptian watercraft (see chapter 6). But, without at least lashing, it is still unclear what would have held the Dahshur boats together in the water. By the Late Bronze Age some Mediterranean shipwrights had begun to dispense with lashings and instead locked their planks together by driving pegs perpendicularly through the tenons of their mortise-and-tenon joints. This practice was known to Egyptian furniture makers as early as the First Dynasty, but there is no evidence that they used it for the hulls of boats or ships before the Persian Period. As they lack an obvious source of structural strength such as lashings or pegged mortise-and-tenon joints, it has been suggested that the Dahshur boats were not working boats at all but merely full-sized models.

A few possible Middle Kingdom boat fragments come from a small port on the Red Sea coast called Marsa Gawasis. Inscriptions in the area report that sailors launched expeditions to Punt there during the reign of Amenemhat II; a unique shrine made of stone anchors was constructed there by Ankhu, an official in the court of Sesostris I. The anchors have a number of words inscribed on them, including the name of 'Punt'.

Unfortunately, the wood from Marsa Gawasis is not very informative. Nothing was found but boards with mortises cut into them; they lack lashing holes or holes for pegs that could have locked tenons in the mortises.

More substantial fragments come from Lisht, an area not far from Cairo where Amenemhat and Sesostris I constructed their pyramids. The boat fragments known have been excavated from the environs of the pyramid of Sesostris I. They seem to come from a very large vessel that was broken up so that its timbers could be used as fill or as foundation material, possibly for ramps used in the construction of the pyramid. A similar ramp or causeway of boat timbers was discovered by Flinders Petrie at the pyramid of Sesostris II at Lahun. Unfortunately, most of the wood was, as Petrie wrote, 'used up' as makeshift excavation equipment.

Fortunately, the Lisht material was better treated. While 76 pieces of wood from the area have been found since 1908, and ten have been drawn, the most revealing is a composite frame built of three timbers. The largest of the three is a 'floor timber', a metre-long curved piece that spanned the bottom of a vessel (figure 17). The other two have been described by the nautical archaeologist Cheryl Haldane as 'upper frames', which rested on each end of the floor timber, leaving a gap in the middle. Was this gap for a stanchion, like those which sit on the frames of the Khufu boat and hold up the central spine? Or are they for a longitudinal, anti-hogging beam of the type indicated in two Early Dynastic models? Until more timbers of this type are found, and their exact location within the ship can be specified, the question is impossible to answer.

The timbers show that frames were in use in at least some vessels of the Middle Kingdom, though different in design from those in the Khufu boats. There seems to have been no use of rail-to-rail lashing through V-shaped holes in the Lisht timbers, the Dahshur boats or the few

17. Internal framing from a Middle Kingdom ship, reused during the construction of the pyramid of Sesostris I at Lisht. (Photograph courtesy of the Metropolitan Museum of Art.)

fragments from Marsa Gawasis; yet this practice may have been in use throughout Egyptian history, since Herodotus may have seen boats being built with the technique in the fifth century BC, as will be explained further in chapter 6. While there was no use of pegs driven perpendicularly through mortise-and-tenon joints, there is evidence from the Lisht timbers that pegs were driven into mortises alongside tenons, to help tighten the joint.

As the internal construction of Egyptian boats evolved from the Old Kingdom to the Middle Kingdom, so did the overall shape of hulls and the rigging that powered them. The bipod mast disappeared entirely in the Middle Kingdom, and by this time all booms were held aloft by lifts. These lifts were generally secured somewhere on the mast below the upper yard; by the time of the New Kingdom lifts for both the upper and lower yards were secured to rings at the masthead.

The variety of ships that were used in the Middle Kingdom can be seen in both tomb models and paintings. One unusually complete set of models comes from the tomb of Meket-Re, an official in the court of the Eleventh Dynasty king Mentuhotep II. His tomb is notable for its many models of daily life, among which the most impressive are the twelve model boats (figures 18 and 19). The models illustrate four types: travelling boats, kitchen boats, yachts and papyrus fishing craft. These twelve models probably represented Meket-Re's personal fleet of pleasure and working craft. Most have miniature figures of Meket-Re sitting, watching his henchmen paddling, rowing or working the rigging — or else engaging in activities like cooking, fishing and fowling.

The four travelling boats and two kitchen boats are essentially the same hull type, a spoon shape with stern slightly higher than the bow. The single steering oars are mounted directly astern. Painted details include a central spine and deck beams. The masts of the models have mast partners at deck level to support them, and the central spine directly behind the mast partner is slotted to allow the mast to be swung back and unstepped (figure 19). The rigging of one of the travelling boats is carefully done, with a number of lifts holding up the boom and yard arm (figure 20). The mast is supported by a backstay, forestay and shrouds, or lateral stays; these are not often represented in Egyptian depictions of boats in any medium. The upper yard was raised, lowered and supported by eight halyards. Other ropes served to set the sail at the proper angle to the wind. The sail itself is made of linen, which seems to have been the usual sailcloth of real Egyptian boats.

The sporting boats are of essentially the same type as the travelling boats and kitchen tenders, though they seem smaller and the sterns are truncated. All have mast partners and slotted central spines, though none has a mast. Meket-Re's yachts had a papyriform shape highly

18. One of Meket-Re's travelling boats. (Photograph courtesy of the Metropolitan Museum of Art. MMA 20.3.2.)

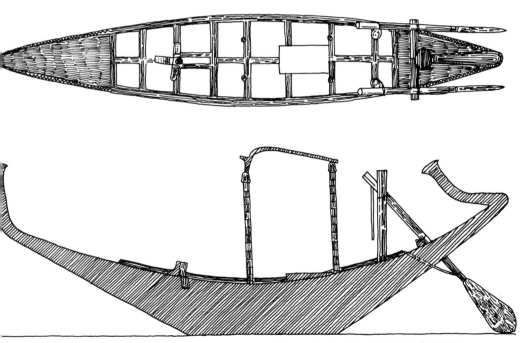

19. Side and top views of one of Meket-Re's yachts. (Drawing by Harold Dinkel after H. E. Winlock, *Models of Daily Life in Ancient Egypt from the Tomb of Meket-Re at Thebes* [Cambridge, Massachusetts, 1955], plate 79.)

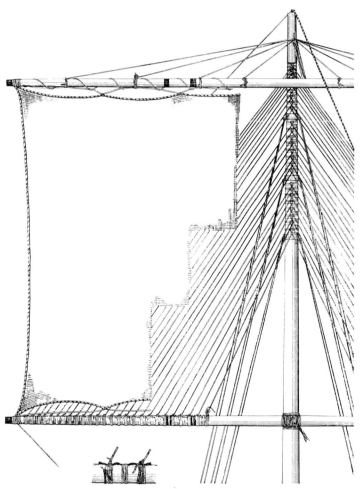

20. Details of the rigging of one of Meket-Re's travelling boats. (From Winlock, *Models of Daily Life*, plate 71. Reproduced courtesy of the Metropolitan Museum of Art.)

reminiscent of the Khufu boat's profile, a straight bow post and a curved stern post. One of the four was fitted with a mast, though not a sail or full rigging, and the others are being paddled. The yachts have two steering oars each, one mounted on each of the boats' quarters. The painted deck beams and central spine are essentially the same as those of the travelling boats and kitchen tenders, indicating that the real vessels

21. A travelling boat scene from the tomb of Khnumhotep at Beni Hasan. (Drawing by Harold Dinkel after P. E. Newberry, *Beni Hasan Part I* [London, 1893], plate XXIX.)

all had similar internal constructional features.

The profile of Meket-Re's travelling boats is similar to boats such as one depicted in the tomb of Khnumhotep at Beni Hasan (figure 21). The hulls seem more finely proportioned, however, which seems to show that Meket-Re's model builder, like nearly all Egyptian model builders of the Middle Kingdom, exaggerated the depth of the boats' hulls. A rigged ship from Khnumhotep's tomb is shown towing a barge on a ritual voyage to Abydos (figure 22). This painting seems deliberately simplified — the boat has far fewer lifts supporting the boom than does the comparable model from Meket-Re's tomb and omits the halyards for the yard. All such boats recall the profiles of a number of Late Bronze Age boats found in a fresco on the Greek island of Thera (figure 23). Those ships also have characteristic Egyptian rigging. Was there a connection between the nautical developments in Egypt and the Aegean? Recent excavations in the Delta show that Aegeans were coming to Egypt regularly, and indeed living there, as early as the Second Intermediate Period.

22. A sailing boat and barge scene from the tomb of Khnumhotep at Beni Hasan. (Drawing by Harold Dinkel after Newberry, *Beni Hasan I*, plate XXIX.)

23. Sailing boat on a fresco at Thera. (From S. Marinatos, *Thera VI* [Athens, 1974], colour plate 9. Reproduced courtesy of the Athenian Archaeological Society.)

In any event, Khnumhotep's tomb has a wealth of other nautical representations, including large travelling boats being paddled upstream, men fishing from a small sporting boat, and even a boat under construction. This last shows men building a boat in exactly the fashion described by Herodotus in the fifth century BC, with short planks laid in a brick-like pattern (figure 24).

At least one tomb from the Middle Kingdom shows warriors fighting from boats (figure 25). The Eleventh Dynasty tomb of Intef at Thebes

24. Boat-construction scene from the tomb of Khnumhotep at Beni Hasan. (Drawing by Harold Dinkel after Newberry, *Beni Hasan I*, plate XXIX.)

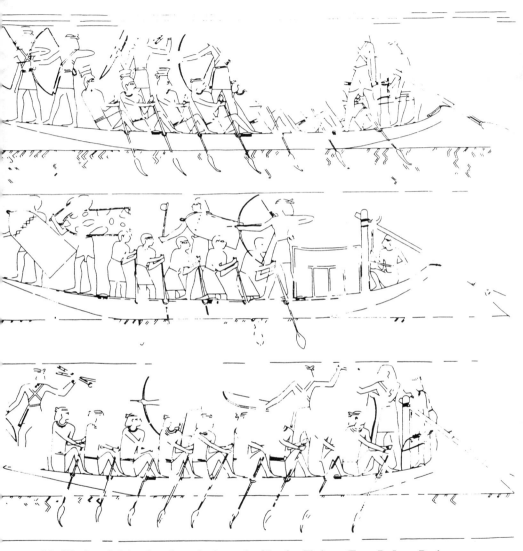

25. Warriors fighting from boats in the tomb of Intef at Thebes. (From B. Jaros-Deckert, *Das Grab des Jny-jtj.f, Die Wandmalereien der XI Dynastie*, Grabung im Asasif 1963-70, Band V, Archäologische Veröfentlichungen 12, Deutsches Archäologisches Institut, Abteilung Kairo [Mainz am Rhein, 1984], plate 14. Reproduced courtesy of the German Institute of Archaeology, Cairo.)

has three warships pictured in it, each of which is shown to be unusually long and low. Did the artist faithfully represent a canoe-like vessel designed for maximum speed or simply show the ship with extra length to accommodate the troops, given the shape of the space he wanted to fill? The enemy is not indicated in this scene, but other scenes in the tomb show Egyptian troops fighting one another, and Egyptian land troops besieging an Asiatic town.

How large were Middle Kingdom boats? No autobiographical reports like Weni's give precise dimensions. The tale of the Shipwrecked Sailor gives dimensions that seem fantastic, though of more or less believable proportion: his ship is said to have been 120 cubits in length and 40 at the beam, or more than 60 metres by 20 metres. The accounts of the dockyards of Sesostris I do not mention any sizes of the ships that were being built or repaired. In one instance, the accounts mention that an *imu* boat has a crew of thirty men, though it is not quite certain whether the thirty men are to crew one or more boats. The accounts also seem to mention another *imu* boat that needed sixty oars. This might suggest a vessel of something over 30 metres long, given 1 metre per rower and thirty rowers per side.

5
The New Kingdom

In the New Kingdom Egypt became an empire of international importance. It dominated Syria-Palestine, challenged the Hittites of Anatolia (modern Turkey) and traded with mainland Greece, the Aegean islands and the Horn of Africa. Colossal building projects within Egypt called for the quarrying and transport of huge amounts of stone. Ships were indispensable to all of this activity.

Also at the beginning of the New Kingdom, for the first time since the Late Predynastic to early Old Kingdom period, it can be seen what ships looked like in the rest of the eastern Mediterranean. At the very beginning of the period the ships of Greece, Crete and Syria-Palestine all seem very similar to their Egyptian counterparts. But it seems clear that near the end of the Eighteenth Dynasty technological developments in the rest of the eastern Mediterranean were making Egypt's traditional nautical practices obsolete. It remains unclear to what extent Egyptian boatbuilders remained conservative in their techniques, and to what extent they adopted new ways of doing things.

There are a large number of sources of information about boats and ships in the New Kingdom but, unfortunately, no archaeological remains of actual boats. Tomb paintings and reliefs of the Eighteenth Dynasty show a wealth of boat representations. Many of these are in funerary contexts, but others show working vessels of daily life, both Egyptian and foreign. Reliefs at two temples are of great importance. The Eighteenth Dynasty queen Hatshepsut's mortuary temple at Deir el-Bahri contains fragmentary scenes of a gigantic barge transporting obelisks, as well as better-preserved images of sea-going craft used to trade with Punt. In the nearby Twentieth Dynasty temple at Medinet Habu a fascinating naval battle between Egyptians and the invading Sea Peoples is portrayed. Numerous other temple reliefs show religious ceremonies with sacred barques. Other boats are portrayed on painted papyrus, sketched on flakes of stone or scratched haphazardly on the walls of buildings or on desert cliffs and boulders.

Textual material from the New Kingdom includes the dockyard records of the Eighteenth Dynasty Pharaoh Tuthmosis III, as well as a pair of actual ship's logs. A number of brief historical inscriptions and business records refer to the use of ships for trade and warfare and a handful of legal documents illustrate the legal status of private and temple-owned ships. A hieroglyphic inscription from the time of the Nineteenth Dynasty Pharaoh Merneptah, as well as cuneiform texts from Palestine and Anatolia, suggests that Egypt was exporting grain by sea to its vassals in Syria-Palestine and its allies the Hittites, although it is unclear whose ships carried the commodity. Finally, for the very end of the Twentieth Dynasty, there is the Report of Wenamun, a detailed account of a voyage from Egypt to Byblos to secure timber and transport it back to Egypt. Models are of minimal importance. The largest single collection is that from Tutankhamun's tomb, but they are far less informative than the Middle Kingdom models from Meket-Re's tomb.

Unfortunately, there is little direct evidence for constructional practices in the Egyptian New Kingdom. In the mid Eighteenth Dynasty reliefs from the temple of Hatshepsut at Deir el-Bahri show her sea-going ships on the way to Punt and her obelisk barges to have hogging trusses, familiar from Old Kingdom ships. This could mean that those ships had no true keels and were still flat-bottomed, much like the Khufu ship. Most models from the period also have flat bottoms, though there is sometimes a thickened bottom plank that projects at the bow and stern. Whether they were still sewn in the manner of Old Kingdom ships is less certain. There are no longer many boat-construction scenes in Egyptian tomb paintings. Those that do exist do not show men lashing hulls together, but neither do they give much insight into constructional techniques at all. If it is true that Herodotus watched Egyptian shipbuilders lashing their vessels together in more or less the same manner as the builders of the Khufu boat, then rail-to-rail lashing may still have been practised in the New Kingdom.

On the other hand, during the late Eighteenth and early Nineteenth Dynasties other Mediterranean peoples made substantial advances in hull construction. It is difficult to believe that Egyptian technology did not develop at all in the thousand years from the Old Kingdom to the New Kingdom, but there is no evidence for what that development might have been.

The New Kingdom sailing ship *par excellence* is a vessel from a scene in the tomb of Rekhmire (figure 26), a high official during the reigns of Tuthmosis III and Amenophis II. The shape of the sail is considerably broader than that of most Old Kingdom sailing vessels. The vessel's rigging is shown in great detail, though some elements are missing. Two lifts hold up the broad yard, which is actually two overlapping spars. One can see how they are lashed together on either side of the masthead. The boom, as well, is made up of two pieces. Numerous lifts hold up the lower yard, which is also lashed to the mast. It is clear that these lifts are not manoeuvrable in any way but serve strictly to hold up the boom. Missing from the picture are the slack lines that would have supported the upper yard when it was lowered. Also missing are sheets or braces that would have controlled the angle of the sail. A relief from the time of Herihor shows how such sails were

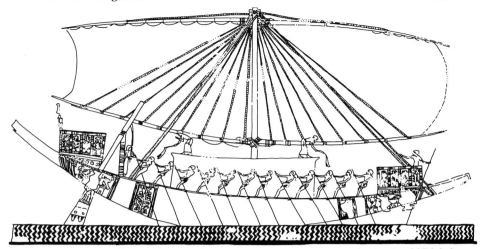

26. Sailing vessel depicted in the tomb of Rekhmire at Thebes. (Drawing by Harold Dinkel after N. de G. Davies, *The Tomb of Rekh-Mi-Re* at Thebes II, Egyptian Expedition Publications volume XI – Plates [New York, 1943], plate LXVIII.)

furled. The upper yard was lowered to a level that was convenient for men standing on the lower yard. Those men detached the foot of the sail and furled the sail to the upper yard by hand. Then the upper yard was lowered the rest of the way.

Rekhmire's vessel is equipped for rowing; it can be seen how standing men strain at their oars under the lash of two coxswains who stand on top of the deck house. But such simultaneous rowing and sailing was probably rare. Egyptians sailed southward with the prevailing north wind and rowed northward, coasting on the current. The fact that such ships were routinely rowed shows that Egyptian sailors probably had not yet perfected any reliable means of tacking, or sailing against a contrary wind. The broad sail is probably also an indication of this, since for sailing upwind with a square sail a tall sail is much more effective than a broad one.

Similar broad sails are seen on the ships of Hatshepsut which sailed to Punt (figure 27). Yet this presents a puzzle. If it is correct that such ships were hard pressed to sail upwind, then the 3900 km round trip to Punt (probably the Horn of Africa) must have been difficult. More precisely, the outward voyage south through the Red Sea would have been easy enough, since the wind blows from the north nearly all year. It is the return trip that would have been difficult, because the winds in the Red Sea north of the latitude of Jiddah in modern Saudi Arabia are almost constantly from the north. To complete the journey, sailors would

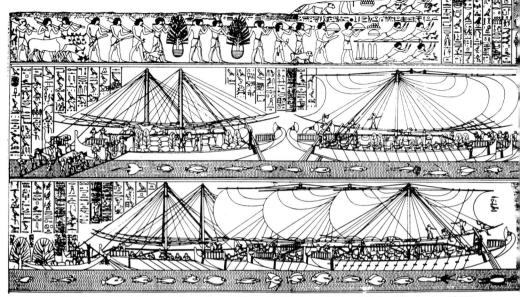

27. Queen Hatshepsut's Punt fleet. (From E. Mariette, *Deir el-Bahari* [Leipzig, 1877], plate 6.)

have had to rely on laborious, inefficient tacking or else row 800 km back to their home port. This is perhaps why Hatshepsut's ships seem to be narrow rowing vessels, rather than beamy merchantmen like the Syrian ships depicted in the tomb of Kenamun, who was mayor of Thebes in the reign of Amenophis III.

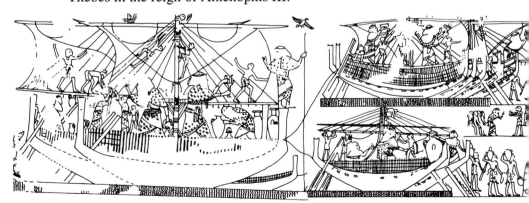

28. Syrian ships in port in the Eighteenth Dynasty tomb of Kenamun. (Drawing by Harold Dinkel after Nina Davies, *Private Tombs at Thebes Volume IV, Scenes from Some Theban Tombs* [Oxford, 1963], plate XV.)

The sea-going ships shown in Kenamun's tomb (figure 28) were rigged much like the Egyptian vessels of the day; indeed, ships depicted in Crete, the Cyclades and mainland Greece all seem to have used the typical 'Egyptian' rig of the early New Kingdom. How those ships were constructed is not known. A shipwreck from the Late Bronze Age, found off a peninsula called Ulu Burun, Turkey, has a keel plank and pegged mortise-and-tenon joints, unlike the Egyptian ships familiar from the Old and Middle Kingdoms but very like the ships of the later Greeks and Romans. This ship was possibly from the eastern Mediterranean, perhaps Syria, Cyprus or Greece, and could be an example of a ship that was essentially like those of the Kenamun painting. If it was, it shows that ships with advanced hulls continued to follow ancient traditions in their rigging.

On the other hand, the Ulu Burun wreck is fifty to one hundred years later than the Syrian ships shown in Kenamun's tomb, which perhaps represent the last gasp of the old tradition. For during the reigns of Amenophis III and Akhenaten there is considerable evidence for new developments in nautical practices in the eastern Mediterranean. During the reign of Amenophis III a new word for ship, *menesh*, occurs for the first time — a word that seems to have referred to a new type of ocean-going vessel. Inscriptions from the time of Amenophis III also show that Egypt was then in contact with the Aegean region: the names of Mycenae and perhaps even Troy were found in his mortuary temple at Thebes. From the end of the reign of Amenophis III and the beginning of the reign of Akhenaten, the first mention is made of new ethnic groups, people like the Sherden, Lukka and Danu who appear later as enemies of Egypt called 'Peoples of the Sea'.

In Akhenaten's reign the first pictorial evidence of a new kind of rigging, the advanced brailed sail, appears. Like the pegged mortise-and-tenon joints found on the Ulu Burun wreck, the brailed sail was typical of Greek and Roman ships in the classical world (figure 29). In the description of the American scholar Lionel Casson, brails were ropes that worked essentially like the cords of a Venetian blind. The brails were secured to the bottom of the sail, then run up through metal rings sewn directly into the sailcloth itself. The lines were then looped over the yard arm and finally led down to deck level, where they could be controlled by sailors. This arrangement made sails easier to handle. Perhaps more importantly, brails permitted sailors to shape their sails in such a way that their ships could tack against the wind. These developments could be related and could mean that new methods of constructing and rigging ships were connected with the appearance of seafaring people from the north-east Mediterranean. The picture remains unclear.

The idea that brailed sails were a foreign innovation receives some

6
The Late and Graeco-Roman Periods

With the end of the New Kingdom Egyptian independence was gradually eroded, as foreign rulers from Libya, Kush, Assyria, Persia, Macedonia and Rome established themselves one after another as masters of Egypt. Egypt relied more than ever on foreign ships, principally Greek, to carry its products abroad, to the Levant, Europe, sub-Saharan Africa, Arabia and India. Archaeological evidence from the Graeco-Roman

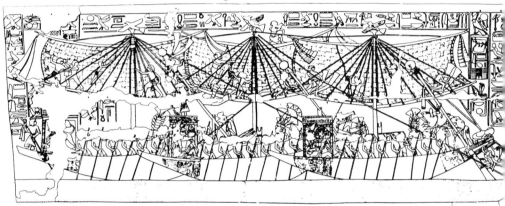

33. Opet Festival procession of Herihor. (From *The Temple of Khonsu Volume 1, Scenes of King Herihor in the Court*, University of Chicago Oriental Institute Publications volume 100 [Chicago, 1979], plate 20. Reproduced courtesy of the Oriental Institute of the University of Chicago.)

Period points to the acceptance of new boatbuilding methods. Textual evidence is mixed. Some material points towards traditional boatbuilding methods, and some suggests the acceptance of innovation.

At the beginning of the Twenty-first Dynasty riverboats seem still to resemble their New Kingdom prototypes. A great scene at Karnak from the reign of King Herihor (figure 33) shows riverboats that could be taken from a New Kingdom relief, and perhaps they were. These boats seem completely uninfluenced by the innovations known to have begun no later than the reign of Akhenaten. Moreover, the composition itself could well be anachronistic, based on a similar scene from the reign of Tutankhamun. Thus, it is unclear whether traditional Nilotic boats continued to ply the river or whether the innovative techniques first seen under Akhenaten had become standard practice as the New Kingdom ended.

Unfortunately, there are rather few depictions of working boats in Egypt after the end of the New Kingdom. Some graffiti in the deserts of Upper Egypt show what are probably ships with the new brailed rig: they are shown with their yards hoisted and lines coming down and gathered amidships (figure 34). The date of these representations is hard to pinpoint, but they seem likely to be from some time after the end of the New Kingdom. Fortunately, from the fifth century BC we have both a complete Egyptian boat and the detailed descriptions of Egyptian boatbuilding recorded in the *History* of Herodotus. Interestingly, these

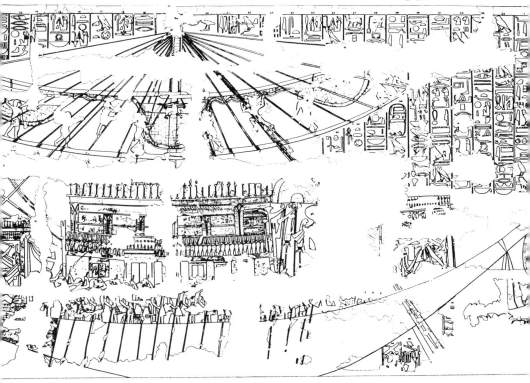

do not seem entirely consistent with one another. The surviving boat was discovered in 1987 buried near the Egyptian town of Matariya near Heliopolis. From preliminary reports it appears that the boat was 11 metres long, 4 metres wide and 1.2 metres deep. The vessel was built of short thick planks of local sycamore and had much of the spoon shape of the Dahshur boats. Unlike the Dahshur boats, however, the boat had to make a vessel that could withstand a great deal of strain — three layers of through-beams tie the hull together, and a complex array of hogging trusses holds up the ends.

As in earlier periods of Egyptian history, ships were used for warfare. At the beginning of the Eighteenth Dynasty the Pharaoh Kamose recorded using riverboats to transport his troops to fight the Hyksos, Palestinian invaders who had ruled northern Egypt for the previous hundred years. A stela found at Gebel Barkal in Nubia records that during an invasion of Syria Tuthmosis III fabricated boats to ferry his army from one side of the Euphrates river to the other. It is possible that this refers to the assembly of prefabricated boats that had been carried in pieces by the army. A vessel built like the Khufu boat could be disassembled and reassembled with very few special tools.

If Egypt's naval power in the Eighteenth Dynasty was built on its own ships, a proposition strongly favoured by scholars like Tgorny Säve-Söderbergh, it seems likely that by the end of the New Kingdom Egypt relied on foreigners for its naval defence. As early as the reign of Ramesses II there are reports that the 'Sherden of the Sea', piratical raiders who may have given their name to Sardinia, had been defeated and impressed into Pharaoh's service. By the reign of Ramesses III it seems likely that a large part of the Egyptian navy was a mercenary force.

At Medinet Habu Ramesses III commemorated his great land and sea campaigns against the invading Sea Peoples (figure 32). The scenes of land fighting, as well as the accompanying texts, show that Sherden mercenaries fought alongside Egyptian troops against a force of Peleset (Philistines), Danu (Homer's Danaans?) and the unidentified Tjeker, Shekelesh and Weshesh, who had destroyed all opposition from Hatti (Anatolia) to Palestine. Sherden are not mentioned among the invaders, but the dress of some of the invaders matches portrayals of Sherden in other reliefs, and it is safe to conclude that they were part of the invasion force.

The ships on both sides of the sea battle are rigged alike, with brailed sails such as those seen for the first time under Akhenaten. The marines on the Egyptian ships wear kilts that are exactly like their opponents'; perhaps this shows that they are Sherden mercenaries such as those shown aiding the Egyptian troops in the land fighting. The ship types described in the inscription accompanying the scene include the *menesh* ships first seen under Amenophis III, *bar* ships and *aha* ships. *Aha* is from a good Egyptian root meaning 'to fight'. The etymologies of the words *menesh* and *bar* are uncertain, but it seems fairly clear that at least *bar* is a non-Egyptian word; it is spelled in a way that indicates it is foreign, and ships of that name are also mentioned in cuneiform texts from Ugarit in Syria. Thus the ship types, the ships' rigging and the dress of their crews strongly hint (but do not prove) that Ramesses III repelled the Sea Peoples' naval armada with his own force of privateer Sea People.

Bar ships and *menesh* ships are mentioned again at the very end of the Twentieth Dynasty, in a literary composition called the Tale (or Report) of Wenamun. Wenamun was a priest of the god Amun who had been sent to the port of Byblos on the Syro-Palestinian coast to secure wood for Amun's sacred river barge. Throughout the tale, Wenamun is forced to depend on foreigners for his transport, either Canaanites or Tjekker (now firmly ensconced in Syria-Palestine). It is interesting that Byblos ships do not occur in this story at all, though the centre of most of the action is Byblos. Instead, *bar* is the common word for ship. And strangely, the common word for ship's captain is *heri-meneshu*, or 'one who is over *menesh* ships'. This has led the scholar Hans Goedicke to conclude that *menesh* referred not to a ship's type but to its status — perhaps a ship chartered by the Egyptian government. Neither Wenamun nor any other Egyptian is ever seen to have direct control over any sea-going vessel; Mediterranean traffic seems to be monopolised by foreigners. At one point this leaves a helpless Wenamun to make the strained argument that any ship chartered by Egypt is, by definition, an Egyptian vessel.

32. The relief at Medinet Habu of the naval battle against the Sea People. (From *Earlier Historical Records of Ramses III*, University of Chicago Oriental Institute Publications VIII, Medinet Habu volume I, plate 37. Reproduced courtesy of the Oriental Institute of the University of Chicago.)

29. Amarna-period boat from Hermopolis showing a sail brailed into a fore-and-aft configuration. (From the Stéphane Cattaui collection. Drawing by Harold Dinkel.)

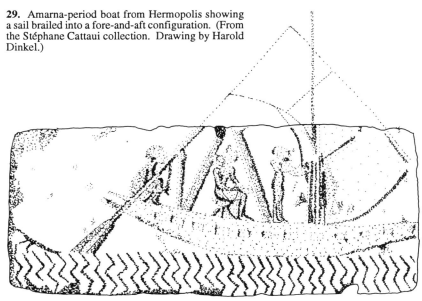

support, however, from a late Eighteenth Dynasty relief from Saqqara, which shows a sea-going ship with a brailed sail discharging amphorae of Canaanite type (figure 30). About the same time foreigners had established small trading colonies on the Mediterranean coast of Egypt. One such has been found at Marsah Matruh, halfway between Alexandria and the modern border between Egypt and Libya. These merchants, who have not been identified, brought with them small ceramic vessels from Cyprus and larger storage amphorae from Syria-Palestine. Perhaps these same traders occasionally came up the Nile to trade in Egypt proper. It is possible that this relief is a record of one of those visits, and that Egyptians learned the technology from them through such contact.

On the Nile itself river traffic continued much as it had for centuries. Local rivermen were important enough to the national economy for the last Pharaoh of the Eighteenth Dynasty, Horemheb, to make special provision for their protection in a decree he issued reforming the taxation system in Egypt. Even though a few reliefs show ships with advanced rigging, most representations show traditional boats. In one scene dating from the time of Tutankhamun local boats with hogging trusses appear, which indicates that they were probably built according to ancient traditions (figure 31).

The building projects of the New Kingdom required huge amounts of stone to be hauled from one place to another and boats of all sizes seem

30. Eighteenth Dynasty relief from Saqqara of a boat with a brailed sail discharging cargo. (Drawing by Harold Dinkel. Berlin 24025.)

31. Riverboats with hogging trusses from the tomb of Huy. (Drawing by Harold Dinkel after A. H. Gardiner and N. de G. Davies, *The Tomb of Huy, Viceroy of Nubia in the Reign of Tutankhamun* [No. 40] [London, 1926], plate XXXII.)

to have been used. Construction records from Thebes show that during the construction of Ramesses II's mortuary temple blocks of stone ranging in size from 3 to 10 cubic cubits (0.45 to 1.5 cubic metres) were delivered in lots of five to seven. Large stones required special barges, like the obelisk lighter of Hatshepsut. This vessel is shown carrying two obelisks end to end, although many authors believe the real ship most likely carried them side by side. Special care seems to have been taken

Egyptian Boats and Ships

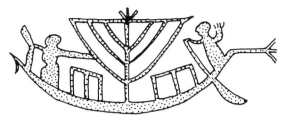

internal frames and was held together with pegged mortise-and-tenon joints.

From about this same time Herodotus gives us a detailed description (Book 2, Chapter 96) of Egyptian *báris* boats (a term probably derived from the *bar* boats of the later New Kingdom):

'But their boats, with which they haul cargo, are made out of acacia, which is similar to Cyrenian lotus and has gummy sap. Cutting 2 cubit [about 1 metre] planks out of these acacias, they build the ship brick-fashion in this manner: they pound down the 2 cubit planks on to large, close-set tenons. When they have completed the hull in this way, they install beams on top. They do not use frames; rather, they bind the joints within using papyrus. They make a single steering oar, which penetrates the keel (-plank). They use an acacia mast, and papyrus sails.'

From this it seems that many Egyptian boatwrights continued to build their ships much as their pharaonic ancestors had: with short lengths of inferior local wood, very probably lashed together. The lack of frames recalls the Dahshur boats, though many Egyptian boats did have frames, perhaps as early as the Early Dynastic Period (and certainly by the Old Kingdom). The description of Egyptians 'binding' their ships from the inside is interesting. Herodotus uses here a Greek verb, *paktoûn*, that has usually been translated as 'to calk' but also has the common meaning 'to bind'. If it is that latter meaning he has in mind, then some boatwrights in the fifth century BC were continuing to lash their vessels together from the inside much as the builders of the Khufu boat did around 2650 BC. This interpretation seems the more likely since Herodotus mentions this interior binding in connection with the vessels' lack of frames. The apparent meaning is that this binding is a substitute for solid wooden framing.

The differences between Herodotus' *báris* and the Matariya boat are worth noting: Herodotus' *báris* boats are made of acacia, while the Matariya boat is made of sycamore. The *báris* boat lacks internal frames, and Herodotus suggests that it is lashed together. The Matariya boat has frames and is put together with pegged mortise-and-tenon joints. Even from Herodotus, however, one can gather that alongside

the traditional methods used by *báris* boatbuilders others were using more advanced techniques. In Book 2, Chapter 36, Herodotus compares Egyptian nautical practices to those of other peoples:
> 'Others fasten the sails' fairleads [*kríkoi*] and brails [*káloi*] outside, but the Egyptians fasten them inside.'

This passage makes it clear that at least some Egyptian boats were rigged with brails, though on the 'inside', that is the windward side of the sail, as opposed to the usual Mediterranean practice of putting them on the 'outside', or forward side. Most likely, the boats with brails are not *báris* boats. In his description of *báris* boats, Herodotus goes on to mention that native Egyptian boats had papyrus sails and usually drifted with the current when they wished to travel against the wind. He makes no mention of brails.

Moreover, some texts from Graeco-Roman Egypt mention *ploîa hellénika*, or 'Greek boats'. The scholar Lionel Casson has speculated that this refers to boats built in the Graeco-Roman manner, as opposed to the native Egyptian tradition. It could be that some conservative (and poor) Egyptians had continued to maintain the old traditions, and that other boatmen, either native or foreign, used more modern techniques.

Foreigners had begun to assume ever growing importance in the seventh century BC, when Kings of Egypt began using Greeks as mercenaries, and a Greek merchant colony was established at Naucratis in the Delta. About the same time, the Egyptian Pharaoh Necho II hired Phoenician navigators to try to circumnavigate Africa; they apparently succeeded. Herodotus reports that the Phoenicians also built Necho a number of warships, probably in the Mediterranean fashion. Necho's concern with trade led him to try to build a canal through the Wadi Tumilat linking the Nile with the Red Sea, a project which was finished by Darius I after the Persian empire conquered Egypt in the late sixth century BC.

By the second century BC Greek sailors used the harbour of Berenike on the Red Sea as a home port from which to trade with Arabia, sub-Saharan Africa and India. Quseir also continued in use, and fragmentary inscriptions found in the area show that Indian sailors made the voyage as well as seamen of Greek or Roman origin. Most of the ships involved in this trade were built in the solid Mediterranean tradition, since they had to brave monsoon winds to sail back and forth across the Indian Ocean. From the time of Egypt's absorption by the Roman Empire in the first century BC huge ships plied back and forth between Egypt and Italy, carrying grain to feed the Roman mob. The principal port for this was Alexandria, founded after Alexander the Great's conquest of Egypt in 332 BC, and widely regarded as the most important port in the eastern Mediterranean.

9
Museums

Most museums with Egyptian collections have at least one boat model. The museums listed here contain the major objects described in the text. Intending visitors are advised to find out the opening times before travelling.

Great Britain

The British Museum, Great Russell Street, London WC1B 3DG. Telephone: 071-636 1555.

The Petrie Museum of Egyptian Archaeology, University College, London, Gower Street, London WC1E 6BT. Telephone: 071-387 7050, extension 2884.

Egypt

Egyptian Antiquities Museum, Tahrir Square, Kasr el-Nil, Cairo.

Solar Barque Museum, Giza.

France

Musée du Louvre, Palais du Louvre, F-75041 Paris.

Germany

Ägyptisches Museum, Staatliche Museen, Bodestrasse 1-3, 102 Berlin.

Italy

Museo Egizio, Palazzo dell'Accademia delle Scienze, Via Accademia delle Scienze 6, Turin.

United States of America

Carnegie Museum of Natural History, 4400 Forbes Avenue, Pittsburgh, Pennsylvania 15213-4080.

Field Museum of Natural History, Roosevelt Road at Lake Shore Drive, Chicago, Illinois 60605.

Metropolitan Museum of Art, 5th Avenue at 82nd Street, New York, NY 10028.

Index

Page numbers in italic refer to illustrations.

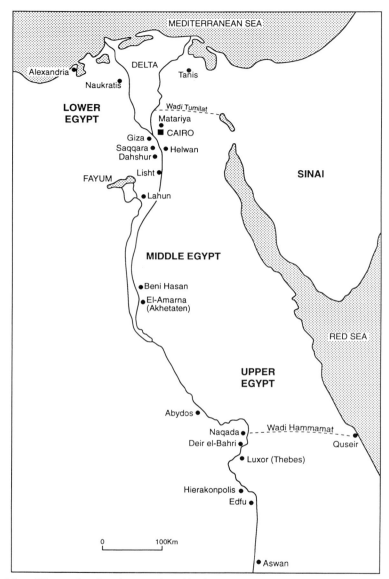

MEDITERRANEAN SEA

DELTA

Alexandria
Naukratis
Tanis

LOWER
EGYPT

Wadi Tumilat

Matariya
CAIRO

Giza
Saqqara • Helwan
Dahshur

Lisht

FAYUM
Lahun

SINAI

MIDDLE EGYPT

Beni Hasan

El-Amarna
(Akhetaten)

RED SEA

UPPER
EGYPT

Abydos

Naqada
Deir el-Bahri
Luxor (Thebes)

Wadi Hammamat

Quseir

Hierakonpolis
Edfu

0   100Km

Aswan

36. Map of Egypt, showing sites mentioned in the text. (Map by Robert Dizon.)

festival of a local Muslim saint, Abu'l Haggag, in Luxor (ancient Thebes) involves carrying a model boat around Luxor Temple. Thus many of the innovations seen for the first time in Egypt — the sail, the mortise-and-tenon joint and mystical and religious imagery based on boats and ships — continued to live on into and even beyond the Middle Ages.

8
Further reading

Arnold, D. *The Pyramid Complex of Senwosret I at Lisht, The South Cemeteries of Lisht Volume III*. Metropolitan Museum of Art Egyptian Expedition, 1992. See the appendix by Cheryl Haldane, 'The Lisht Timbers: A Report on their Significance'.

Bass, G.F. (editor). *A History of Seafaring Based on Underwater Archaeology*. Thames & Hudson, 1972.

Boreux, C. *Études de nautique égyptienne*. Mémores publiés par les membres de l'Institut Français d'Archéologie Orientale du Caire, T. 50, 1925.

Gasson, L. *Ships and Seamanship in the Ancient World*. Princeton University Press, 1971.

Göttlicher, A., and Werner, W. *Schiffsmodelle im alten Ägypten*. Arbeitskreis historischer Schiffbau e.V., 1971.

Jenkins, N. *The Boat Beneath the Pyramid*. Holt, Rinehart and Winston, 1980.

Jones, D. *A Glossary of Ancient Egyptian Nautical Titles and Terms*. Kegan Paul International, 1988.

Jones, D. *Model Boats from the Tomb of Tut^cnkhamun*. Griffith Institute, 1990.

Landström, Björn. *Ships of the Pharaohs*. Doubleday, 1970.

Lipke, P. *The Royal Ships of Cheops*. BAR International Series number 225, 1984.

Patch, D.C., and Haldane, C.W. *The Pharaoh's Boat at the Carnegie*. The Carnegie Museum of Natural History, 1990.

Reisner, G.A. *Models of Ships and Boats*. Catalogue géneral des antiquités égyptiennes du Musée du Caire, numbers 4798-4976 et 5034-5200, Imprimerie de l'Institut Français d'Archéologie Orientale, 1913.

Winlock, H.E. *Models of Daily Life In Ancient Egypt from the Tomb of Meket-Re^c at Thebes*. Harvard University Press, 1955.

7
Boats in Egyptian religion

Unfortunately, there are very few coherent descriptions of Egypt's religious beliefs comparable to the Qur'an, the Bible or the Greek myths. Egyptian religious texts are mostly collections of incantations or ritual recitations. Thus, to get an idea of the place of nautical themes in Egyptian religion, it becomes necessary to draw inferences from artistic representations and chance references in ritual texts.

Religious beliefs connected with boats go back to prehistory. Gerzean Egyptians sometimes buried their dead with pots painted with boats, and the first known Egyptian tomb painting has a boat procession as its principal theme. By the First Dynasty the practice of burying actual boats with the dead was developed.

In the Fourth Dynasty Khufu had several boats buried next to his pyramid at Giza, two of which still exist. A number of other Old Kingdom pyramids also had boats buried next to them. Boats also figure in the Pyramid Texts, the forerunners of the New Kingdom Book of the Dead, which occur for the first time carved on the walls of the burial chamber of the late Fifth Dynasty Pharaoh Unas.

In one of these early texts (Spell 263), Unas is ferried from this world to the next on the 'reed floats of heaven'. The fact that the text specifies reed floats could indicate that these incantations are very old indeed, perhaps earlier than the invention of planked boats.

> 'The reed floats of heaven have been given to Re, that he may
>   cross on them to the horizon;
> The reed floats of heaven have been given to Harakhty, that
>   Harakhty may cross on them to Re;
> The reed floats of heaven have been given to Unas, that he may
>   cross on them to the horizon, to Re;
> The reed floats of heaven have been given to Unas, that he may
>   cross on them to Harakhty, to Re.'

Another possible echo of prehistory is the special barque of the god Sokar, which normally has an unusually high bow post surmounted by an antelope's head ornament (figure 35). This high bow strongly recalls the bow of the black vessel in the Gerzean tomb painting from Hierakonpolis Tomb 100. Much of Egypt's later funerary literature involves nautical themes, with long sections of the Middle Kingdom Coffin Texts (so called because they were written on the coffins of wealthy Egyptians) and the New Kingdom Book of the Dead (usually written on papyrus) making mention of boat parts, some of them obscure.

Perhaps the most commonly represented nautical ritual in Egyptian

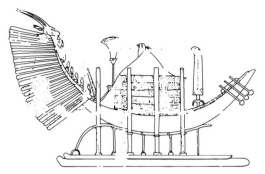

35. A barque of Sokar. (Drawing by Harold Dinkel after *Festival Scenes of Ramses III*, University of Chicago Oriental Institute Publications LI, Medinet Habu volume IV [Chicago, 1940], plate 221.)

religious art was the Abydos pilgrimage. Beginning in the Middle Kingdom, Egyptian tomb paintings include scenes of the deceased being ferried to Abydos to worship Osiris, god of the dead. When such scenes appear at Thebes, they generally show the deceased on a boat with its sails furled, heading north to Abydos, then with its sail deployed on the southward return journey. Whether such pilgrimages were actually made is unknown. It could be that the actual practice involved only sending votive gifts to Abydos; it could be that the painting itself was considered an adequate substitute.

Boats figured prominently in many Egyptian festivals and rituals. Most gods had sacred boats, some only models, some actual vessels that sailed about on the river. Numerous reliefs in Egyptian temples show priests carrying such model boats around during festivals or sailing the boats of major divinities like Amun. Major temple complexes include 'barque shrines', where model boats were carried and temporarily deposited in symbolic voyages. The late Twentieth Dynasty Report of Wenamun tells of a priest of Amun travelling to Byblos to get cedar wood for the river barge of Amun. Penniless, he offers life and health on Amun's behalf to the prince of Byblos in return for the wood. The prince demands and eventually gets payment.

A great 'dramatic' text is recorded at the Ptolemaic temple of Edfu in Upper Egypt. Scenes accompanying the text show the god Horus standing on a boat spearing a hippopotamus who represents his uncle Seth, the enemy of Osiris.

In the Graeco-Roman period the cult of the goddess Isis spread throughout the eastern Mediterranean and, with it, something of the Egyptians' nautical symbolism. Isis was particularly venerated by sailors, since her astral connections made her important to navigation. Apuleius' *Metamorphosis* describes a ritual designed to ensure a safe sailing season that involved consecrating a special barque to Isis. Christian tales from medieval Egypt have angels travelling in boats, and even today the